AF270490
Greetings, cows!
1

MARVELS
ANIMALS 48

COWS

KATE RIGGS

CREATIVE EDUCATION | CREATIVE PAPERBACKS

4

table of contents

Published by Creative Education and Creative Paperbacks
P.O. Box 227, Mankato, Minnesota 56002
Creative Education and Creative Paperbacks
are imprints of The Creative Company
www.thecreativecompany.us

Design by Wyeth Morgan
Art direction by Blue Design (www.bluedes.com)

Images by Dreamstime/Dary423, 24, Vidu Gunaratna, 23; flickr/Biodiversity
Heritage Library, cover (left); Freepik/alirezahbn, 13; Getty Images/
BrandyTaylor, 10–11, George Pachantouris, 14–15, John Lund, 3, 20–21;
Pexels/JacLou- DL, 1, Matthias Zomer, 17; Shutterstock/Alberto Masnovo,
4; Unsplash/Claudio Schwarz, 18-19, David Dvořáček, 16, Jennifer Ermler, 2,
Josua De, cover (middle), Maria Krasnova, 8–9, Serge Le Strat, 6–7, Subtle
Cinematics, cover (right)

Library of Congress Cataloging-in-Publication Data
Names: Riggs, Kate, author.
Title: Cows / Kate Riggs.
Description: Mankato, Minnesota : Creative Education / Creative Paperbacks,
    [2026] | Series: Marvels | Includes bibliographical references and
    index. | Audience: Ages 4-7 | Audience: Grades K-1 | Summary: "An
    introduction to cows, this beginning reader features eye-catching
    photographs, humorous captions, and basic life science facts about these
    grass-loving grazers. Includes a labeled image guide, glossary, and
    further resources";– Provided by publisher.
Identifiers: LCCN 2024044709 (print) | LCCN 2024044710 (ebook) | ISBN
    9798889895732 (library binding) | ISBN 9781682777053 (paperback) | ISBN
    9798889895794 (ebook)
Subjects: LCSH: Cows–Juvenile literature.
Classification: LCC SF197.5 .R54 2026 (print) | LCC SF197.5 (ebook) | DDC
    636.2–dc23/eng/20241213
LC record available at https://lccn.loc.gov/2024044709
LC ebook record available at https://lccn.loc.gov/2024044710

Printed in India

Cows on the farm live in a barn. **Herds** of cows may feed on grasslands.

8

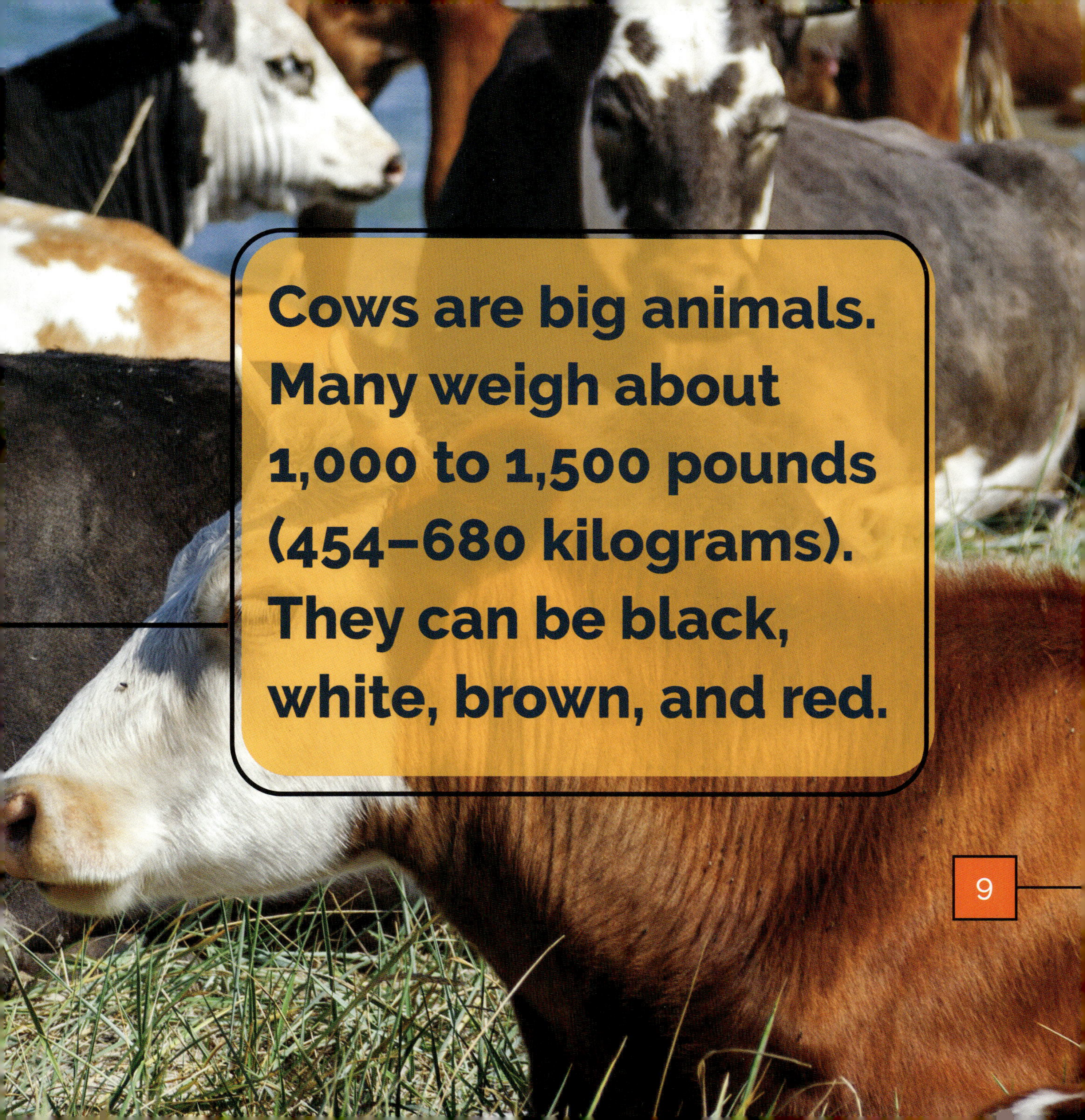

Cows are big animals.
Many weigh about
1,000 to 1,500 pounds
(454–680 kilograms).
They can be black,
white, brown, and red.

9

Dairy cows make a lot of milk. Farmers get the milk from the udder.

DAIRY COWS MAKE 6 TO 7 GALLONS (22.7–26.5 LITERS) OF MILK EACH DAY.

Cows are grass eaters. They eat fresh grass. They eat dried grass. They also eat grains and other plants.

PASS THE
GREENS.

CALVES CAN STAND AND WALK AN HOUR AFTER BIRTH.

Baby cows
called calves
drink milk. Then
they start eating
other foods.

Cows chew grass.
They flick their
tails at bugs.
They find water
to drink.

16

HOLY COW!
18

Farewell, cows!

[Picture a Cow]

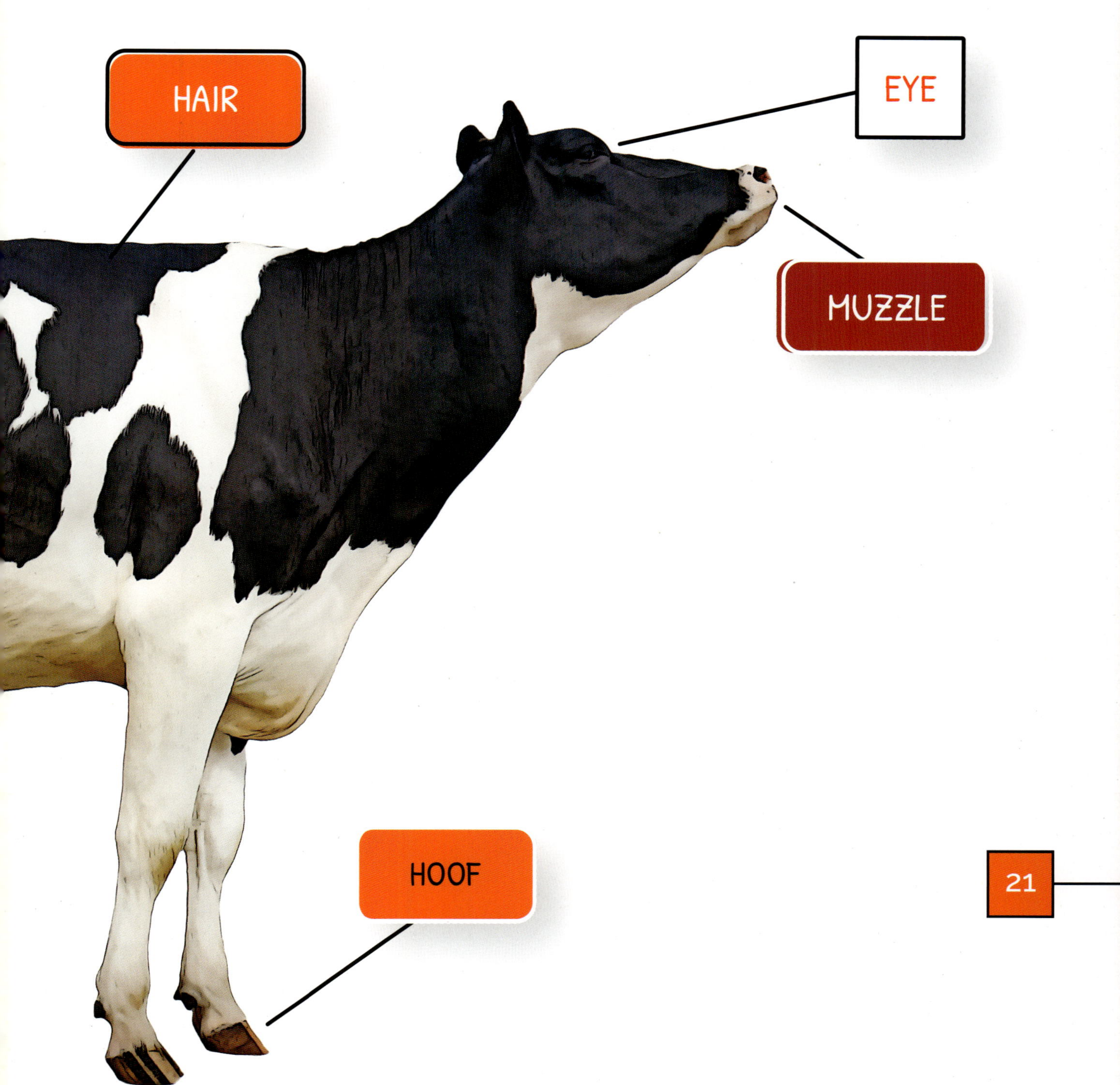

HAIR
EYE
MUZZLE
HOOF
21

WORDS TO KNOW

herd: a group of cows that are kept together

udder: the baglike part of a female cow where milk is made

READ MORE

Mazzarella, Kerri. *Cows.* Coral Springs, Fla.: Seahorse Publishing, 2023.

Rathburn, Betsy. *Cows.* Minneapolis: Bellwether Media, 2024.

WEBSITES

Cattle Facts for Kids
https://kids.kiddle.co/Cattle

Read about different types of cattle, including cows.

Facts About Cows
https://www.aipl.arsusda.gov/kc/cowfacts.html

Learn more about dairy cows in the United States.

23